The Courage of Sarah Noble

Study Guide

by Rebecca Gilleland

For the book by Alice Dalgliesh

Progeny Press

Limited permission to reproduce this study guide

**Purchase of this book entitles an individual teacher
to reproduce pages for use in the classroom or home.
Multiple teachers may not reproduce pages
from the same study guide.**

The Courage of Sarah Noble Study Guide
A Progeny Press Study Guide
by Rebecca Gilleland
edited by Andrew Clausen

Printed in the United States of America.

ISBN 978-1-58609-299-3 Book
       978-1-58609-530-7 CD
       978-1-58609-390-7 Set

Table of Contents

Note to Instructor

How to Use Progeny Press Study Guides.   Progeny Press study guides are designed to help students better understand and enjoy literature by getting them to notice and understand how authors craft their stories and to show them how to think through the themes and ideas introduced in the stories. To properly work through a Progeny Press study guide, students should have easy access to a good dictionary, a thesaurus, a Bible (we use NIV translation, but that is up to your preference; just be aware of some differences in language), and sometimes a topical Bible or concordance. Supervised access to the Internet also can be helpful at times, as can a good set of encyclopedias.

Most middle grades and high school study guides take from eight to ten weeks to complete, generally working on one section per week. Over the years, we have found that it works best if the students completely read the novel the first week, while also working on a prereading activity chosen by the parent or teacher. Starting the second week, most parents and teachers have found it works best to work on one study guide page per day until the chapter sections are completed. Students should be allowed to complete questions by referring to the book; many questions require some cross-reference between elements of the stories.

Most study guides contain an Overview section that can be used as a final test, or it can be completed in the same way the chapter sections were completed. If you wish to perform a final test but your particular study guide does not have an Overview section, we suggest picking a couple of questions from each section of the study guide and using them as your final test.

Most study guides also have a final section of essays and postreading activities. These may be assigned at the parents' or teachers' discretion, but we suggest that students engage in several writing or other extra activities during the study of the novel to complement their reading and strengthen their writing skills.

As for high school credits, most Christian high schools with whom we have spoken have assigned a value of one-fourth credit to each study guide, and this also seems to be acceptable to colleges assessing homeschool transcripts.

Internet References

All websites listed in this study guide were checked for appropriateness at the time of publication. However, due to the changing nature of the Internet, we cannot guarantee that the URLs listed will remain appropriate or viable. Therefore, we urge parents and teachers to take care in and exercise careful oversight of their children's use of the Internet.

Synopsis

This is a true story about a young girl named Sarah Noble. In the year 1707 she goes with her father to cook for him while he builds the first house in New Milford, Connecticut. There are many things to be afraid of along the way, but she always reminds herself to keep up her courage. She does this by holding the red cape her mother had placed around her as she left and repeating her mother's words. "Keep up your courage," her mother had said, fastening the cloak under Sarah's chin. "Keep up your courage, Sarah Noble!" Sarah learns to appreciate the wonderful family she has and the Indians who befriend her. She is very happy when reunited with her mother, father, brothers, and sisters at the end of the book.

About the Author

Alice Dalgliesh was born in 1893 in Trinidad, British West Indies, and grew up there on the tropical island. At nineteen she decided to become a kindergarten teacher because of her interest in writing for children. She came to America and attended Pratt Institute and Teachers College at Columbia University receiving her B.A. and her M.A. at Columbia. She taught in elementary schools for several years, and later taught a course in children's literature at Teachers College. She worked as children's book editor for Charles Scribner's Sons from 1934 until her retirement in 1960.

Alice Dalgliesh was the editor and author of many children's books. She was runner-up for the Newbery Medal in 1945 for *The Silver Pencil,* in 1953 for *The Bears on Hemlock Mountain,* and in 1955 for *The Courage of Sarah Noble.* She died June 11, 1979, in Woodbury, Connecticut.

Background Information

In the early 1700s, most of America was still wilderness. As people built settlements and farmed, some dealt fairly with the Indians while others did not. Always, friendship and courage were an important part of daily life. Sarah Noble did go with her father to cook for him, but most of the details have been filled in by the author.

Before-you-read Activities

1. Define courage in your own words.

2. Look at a United States map and find Connecticut. Describe what you imagine it would be like as total wilderness.

3. Where do people stay now when they travel? What would it be like to knock on a stranger's door and ask for a place to stay?

4. What kinds of homes did the settlers build? What building materials did they use? Who did the building?

5. Indian tribes were all very different from each other. Some were peaceful, some were not. Many tribes fought with each other even when they were friendly to white men. Why are some people peaceful? Why are some warlike?

As-you-read Activity

1. Make a list of the different times throughout the book that Sarah reminds herself to keep up her courage and holds her red cloak. Why does she hold the cloak? What does it remind her of?

Chapters 1 & 2

Vocabulary:

Define these words or phrases and use them in a sentence.

1. settlement _____

   _____

   _____

2. musket _____

   _____

   _____

3. heathen savage _____

   _____

   _____

4. timidly _____

_____

_____

5. fearful _____

_____

_____

Questions:

1. Why do you think Sarah said she would go with her father? Would you have gone? _____

_____

_____

2. Sarah misses her family. Describe two things she remembers about her mother.

_____

_____

_____

3. Read Psalm 4:8. "I will lie down and sleep in peace, for you alone, O Lord, make me dwell in safety." The Lord watches over us while we sleep just like a father watches over his children. Why did Sarah's father stay up all night as she slept? _____

_____

_____

4. The author uses a simile to describe Sarah's mother ". . . clucking and fussing like a mother hen." Later Mistress Robinson began clucking and fussing just as Sarah's mother might have done. What made them different? _____

_____

_____

5. In the second chapter Sarah thinks that the woman's face is not like a mother's face. Why? _____

_____

_____

6. Lemuel and Robert tease Sarah. Why? _____

_____

_____

7. How did Sarah respond? Why? _____

_____

_____

8. Have you ever been teased? How did you respond? Read Matthew 5:38, 39, 44. "You have heard that it was said, 'Eye for eye, and tooth for tooth.' But I tell you, Do not resist an evil person. If someone strikes you on the right cheek, turn to him the other also.' But I tell you: Love your enemies and pray for those who persecute you." How should you respond? _____

_____

_____

_____

_____

Chapters 3 & 4

Vocabulary:

Look closely at the following sentences in the book and decide what the meanings of the underlined words are. Write down your definition. Look the word up in the dictionary and write down this definition also.

1. She had a funny picture in her mind of <u>solemn</u>, long-faced Thomas carefully putting the logs in place.

    Your definition _____

    Dictionary definition _____

2. Now they had come to the top of a long, steep hill and they stopped at a place where there were not many trees, only bushes and <u>coarse</u> grass.

    Your definition_____

    Dictionary definition _____

3. It was a <u>fair</u> piece of land with the trees already cleared.

    Your definition_____

    Dictionary definition _____

4. It was in the hill across the river that Sarah and her father found a place <u>hollowed</u> out, that would do for the night.

   Your definition _____

   Dictionary definition _____

5. Then there came a strange <u>odor</u> that made Sarah choke.

   Your definition _____

   Dictionary definition _____

6. The night sounds <u>wove</u> themselves into a pleasant, comforting pattern.

   Your definition _____

   Dictionary definition _____

Questions:

1. Trusting, Sarah followed her father's voice leading her on. We are to trust our heavenly Father in the same way. Read Psalm 139:7-10. "Where can I go from your Spirit? Where can I flee from your presence? If I go up to the heavens, you are there; if I make my bed in the depths, you are there. If I rise on the wings of the dawn, if I settle on the far side of the sea, even there your hand will guide me, your right hand will hold me fast." Psalm 62:8. "Trust in him at all times, O people; pour out your hearts to him, for God is our refuge." Summarize these verses briefly in your own words. _____

_____

_____

_____

_____

2. Why did Sarah's father say she was too wise for her years?_____

_____

_____

3. Why didn't he shoot the deer? _____

_____

_____

4. Sarah's father said Mistress Robinson should teach her children to watch their words. What does it mean to "watch your words"? _____

_____

_____

5. As Sarah lay and listened to the night sounds she asked herself if she was keeping up her courage or being afraid. Why did she start talking to her father?

_____

_____

6. Sarah was proud that she was keeping up her courage and her father's. Why is it important that they encourage each other? _____

_____

_____

How can you encourage and comfort the people in your family? Be specific.

_____

_____

_____

_____

7.   Read Hebrews 10:24. "And let us consider how we may spur one another on toward love and good deeds." Rewrite this in your own words._____

_____

_____

_____

_____

Chapters 5 & 6

Vocabulary:

Circle the letter of the correct meaning *as it was used in the book.*

1. namesake
   a. a person named after someone
   b. to do something for someone

2. mild
   a. a flavor
   b. gentle

3. palisade
   a. a castle
   b. a fence of sharp wooden stakes

4. petticoat
   a. an underskirt
   b. a jacket

5. serious
   a. earnest, sincere, and solemn
   b. angry, frowning

6. mortar & pestle
    a. coffee grinder
    b. a bowl and stick used to grind things

Questions:

1. Sarah was nervous when her father left to build the house. What did she do to encourage herself?_____

    _____

    _____

2. What is your favorite Bible story? Why? _____

    _____

    _____

3. Why do you think the Indian children gathered around to watch her? _____

    _____

    _____

4. She wished that God would tell her what to do. He did not speak out loud but Sarah suddenly knew what to do. What was it? _____

    _____

    _____

5. At the end of chapter five, Sarah is sorry about something. What was it? _____

_____

_____

6. After she asked her father if she could visit the Indian houses, she waited quietly and patiently for his answer. Would that have been hard to do? Why?

_____

_____

7. What do you think Sarah's reaction would have been if he had said no? Why? Support your answer with at least two reasons. _____

_____

_____

8. How did Sarah honor her father? _____

_____

_____

Read Deuteronomy 5:16, "Honor your father and your mother, as the Lord your God has commanded you, so that you may live long and that it may go well with you in the land the Lord your God is giving you," and Proverbs 23:24, "The father of a righteous man has great joy; he who has a wise son delights in him." In what way can you honor your father and/or mother?

_____

_____

_____

_____

Word Pictures:

A word picture is made by using words that create a picture in your mind or a feeling. They are called *imagery, similes,* and *metaphors.* Finish the sentences.

1. Sarah kept *as still as* _____.

2. The children came in, creeping nearer, creeping nearer, *like* _____

   _____.

3. *Like* _____, the children were off and away.

4. So she went out and filled a basket with the berries, which were *like* _____

   _____.

Chapters 7 & 8

Vocabulary:

Match the word with the correct definition.

1. scarlet ____   a. American Indian woman or wife

2. squaw ____   b. walk with long steps

3. stride ____   c. red

4. eagerly ____   d. go and get

5. fetch ___   e. excitedly and impatiently

Questions:

1. The Indians kept watch on Guarding Hill for the Indians from the north. Why? _____

    _____

    _____

    _____

2. What did her father tell her was the best courage of all? _____

    _____

    _____

3. As Sarah watched her father leave what was she worrying about? _____

    _____

    _____

4. It is said that friends have ways of speaking without words. Do you think this is true? Explain why or why not. _____

    _____

    _____

5. Read Proverbs 17:17. "A friend loves at all times, and a brother is born for adversity." Tall John was Sarah's friend. At the end of Chapter 7, how did he comfort her?_____

    _____

    _____

6. Why were the Indian children so interested in Sarah's hair? What simile did the author use to describe Sarah's hair? _____

    _____

    _____

7. Why did Sarah cry and call it "a lonely business"? _____

_____

_____

8. When Sarah prayed before bed, she did not simply repeat a memorized prayer, but she asked God for what she wanted and needed. Read Ephesians 6:18. "And pray in the Spirit on all occasions with all kinds of prayers and requests. With this in mind, be alert and always keep on praying for all the saints." Also 1 Thessalonians 5:16-18. "Be joyful always; pray continually; give thanks in all circumstances, for this is God's will for you in Christ Jesus." List three different parts of prayer these verses tell us about. _____

_____

_____

_____

_____

_____

Chapters 9, 10 & 11

Vocabulary:

A synonym is another word that has the same meaning. Examples: scarlet=red, resurrection=returned to life, cravat=necktie. Think of synonyms for these words.

1. dew = _____

2. disturbance = _____

3. charming = _____

4. amused = _____

5. stiff = _____

6. tiresome = _____

7. fretful = _____

8. outlandish = _____

9. queer = _____

10. raided = _____

Questions:

1. All at once, Sarah felt the fear in the air. Why were the Indians afraid? _____

    _____

    _____

2. What did she hold as she went to sleep? Why? _____

    _____

    _____

3. Tall John told her that the village would be warned and ready if the Indians from the North were coming. How would the Indians know and warn each other? _____

    _____

    _____

4. During the night she heard wailing. What was it?_____

    _____

    _____

5. What game did she play with the other children? _____

    _____

    _____

6. Why do you think Tall John was looking sadly at her? _____

_____

_____

7. The first thing Sarah did when she saw her family was to kneel and hold the baby. Why?_____

_____

_____

8. The baby was strong now but might not have lived if they'd come earlier. How did Sarah feel about that? _____

_____

_____

9. Was it worth being alone all that time? Explain. _____

_____

_____

10. Sarah's mother "had words with" Sarah's father about leaving Sarah. What does that mean? _____

_____

_____

11. What did her father mean when he said, "She has had to be too much of a woman"? _____

_____

_____

12. Why didn't she need her cloak anymore? _____

_____

_____

13. Once again, define courage in your own words. _____

_____

_____

_____

Activities, Arts and Crafts

Cooking Center:

Sarah's father traded with the Indians for corn. Sarah ground it with a small mortar and pestle to make corn cakes in the ashes. Make cornmeal biscuits to eat in class.

Cornmeal Biscuits
1/3 cup shortening
1 1/4 cups flour
1/2 cup cornmeal
2 1/2 tsp. baking powder
3/4 tsp. salt
3/4 cup milk or water

Instructions: Heat oven to 350 degrees. Mix baking powder and salt into the flour and cornmeal. Cut shortening into the flour mixture. Add just enough milk so the dough leaves the sides of the bowl and forms a ball.

Turn dough out on lightly floured board and knead lightly for 1 minute. Roll 1/2 inch thick. Cut with a butter knife into 2-inch squares. Place about 1 inch apart on an ungreased cookie sheet. Bake until just golden, 9–11 minutes. Remove from cookie sheet immediately. Makes about 1 dozen.

Craft:

Build a pretzel log cabin.

Materials:

40 small stick pretzels per student
2 graham cracker sections per student
Glue: you may use regular craft glue or make the cabin edible by using thick frosting. (2 cups powdered sugar, 1 Tbsp soft butter, milk. Cream sugar and butter. Add milk by drops until frosting is stiff but tacky.) Another option if children will eat them in class is to use cheese spread as your glue.

Give materials to each student. Using 4 pretzel sticks, glue them to the paper plate in a square. Then continue gluing "logs" on until the walls are complete. Carefully put the crackers on top as the roof. Let dry or eat!

Art Project:

Create a picture of Sarah and her father in the forest.

Options:

1. Draw and color.

2. Draw Sarah and her father on white paper. Color and cut out. Draw tree trunks on brown construction paper, leaves on green, red for Sarah's cape, etc. Cut them out and glue onto a piece of construction paper as a collage. Use blue for daytime sky or black as a nighttime sky.

3. Draw Sarah and her father on white paper. Color and cut out. Glue to cardboard and let dry. Cut the figures out. Give each child a 2" × 4" rectangle of red felt to use as Sarah's cape. Glue or sew the red cape on Sarah.

Game:

Play "find the pebble," the game that Sarah played with the Indian children.

Items needed:
1 pebble for each group of 5 or 6 children.

Instructions:
All the children take their shoes off and place them in a row or in the center of a circle. One child begins by hiding his eyes. The rest of the children hide the pebble in a shoe. The first child uncovers his eyes and guesses where the pebble is. Continue around the group until everyone gets a chance to guess where the pebble is. Remind the other children that they can clap and cheer, but must not tell where the pebble is.

Crossword Puzzle

Finish each sentence with the correct word from the following list. Use the words to complete the crossword:

courage   cloak   settlement   trail   latch   cabin   Indians
johnnycake   traded   moccasin   signal   journey   wigwams   waited

Across

2. Once she seemed to hear a long, low wailing. Was this the _____?

4. Sarah _____ for her father to speak.

6. They came at sundown to a _____.

10. "Tonight we do not need to eat that dry _____," Sarah said.

11. She had kept up her _____ and it was something that would always be with her.

13. Were the _____ coming down from the North?

14. Suppose . . . Suppose . . . But tired from long days in the sun she slept at last, always with a fold of her _____ caught in her hand.

Down

1. That she would have to see for herself—if she could even bring herself to look into one of those queer _____.

3. So they were walking, all three of them, when they came to the _____ where the candle wood was lighted early.

5. The _____ was lifted and a woman stood in the doorway looking at them.

7. They _____ with the Indians for corn, and ground it with the small mortar and pestle Thomas had brought in one of the saddle bags.

8. She also made a pair of deerskin _____.

9. It had been a long day, and the _____ through the forest had not been easy.

10. The frost was on the ground when Sarah stood, holding Tall John's hand, to watch her father start on his _____.

12. Tall John's wife taught Sarah how to weave a _____.

Suggestions for Further Reading

Other books by Alice Dalgliesh:

The Thanksgiving Story　　　　　　　ages 5–8, published by Aladdin
　　　　　　　　　　　　　　　　　　　and by Scholastic

The Bears on Hemlock Mountain　　　ages 5–8, published by Aladdin
The Silver Pencil　　　　　　　　　　ages 12 and up, published by Scholastic
The Fourth of July Story　　　　　　　published by Aladdin

Other interesting books:

If You Lived in Colonial Times　　　　by Ann McGovern, grades K–3, published by
　　　　　　　　　　　　　　　　　　　Scholastic

The Long Way to a New Land　　　　by Joan Sandin, grades K–3, published by
　　　　　　　　　　　　　　　　　　　HarperCollins

The Long Way Westward　　　　　　　by Joan Sandin, grades K–3, published by
　　　　　　　　　　　　　　　　　　　HarperCollins

The Josefina Story Quilt　　　　　　　by Eleanor Coerr, grades K–3, published by
　　　　　　　　　　　　　　　　　　　HarperCollins

Sarah, Plain and Tall　　　　　　　　by Patricia MacLachlan, grades 4–6,
　　　　　　　　　　　　　　　　　　　published by HarperCollins

Ox-Cart Man　　　　　　　　　　　　by Donald Hall, grades K–3, published by
　　　　　　　　　　　　　　　　　　　Puffin Books

Kirsten: An American Girl (series)　　by Janet Shaw, grades 2–5, published by
　The American Girls Collection　　　Pleasant Company.
The Sign of the Beaver　　　　　　　by Elizabeth George Speare, grades 5–7, pub-
　　　　　　　　　　　　　　　　　　　lished by Dell

Answer Key

Before-you-read Activities

1. Answers will vary.

2. Answers will vary.

3. Now people stay in motels, inns, and hotels. The rest of the answer will vary.

4. The settlers built many styles of homes. The most common were sod shanties, dugouts and log cabins. Years later as the westward expansion hit the prairies, sod shanties and rough board shacks were the most common. Materials consisted of whatever was easily available, usually logs, wood planks and sod. Settlers either built their own homes or traded labor or goods to have help building their home.

5. Answers will vary.

As-you-read Activity

1. Different times in the book that Sarah holds the cloak and reminds herself to keep up her courage:

   a.   The first night Sarah draws her cloak close.

   b.   She thought about her family, and baking pies and fell asleep holding a fold of the cloak and saying "Keep up your courage Sarah Noble."

   c.   She keeps her cloak on while waiting for her father to come into Mistress Robinson's house.

   d.   She asked for her cloak and held it tightly that night sleeping in Mistress Robinson's house and saying "Keep up your courage, Sarah Noble."

   e.   The first night in the cave, Sarah stayed comfortable wrapped in her warm cloak. She said "Keep up your courage" after the skunk was gone.

   f.   She said "Keep up your courage" each day when she sat alone while her father built the house.

   g.   When Sarah got lonely and had no one, not even her doll, to read to, she got up and got her cloak.

   h.   She told herself to keep up her courage when the Indian children encircled her.

   i.   When her father left, Sarah held Tall John's hand and wrapped her cloak tightly around herself and repeated, "Keep up your courage."

   j.   While she stayed with Tall John's family, she slept always with a fold of her cloak caught in her hand, Before she fell asleep, she said "Keep up your courage."

Why did she hold the cloak, and what did it remind her of?

     Sarah held the cloak for comfort and encouragement. It reminded Sarah of her mother.

Chapters 1 & 2

Vocabulary:

1. settlement = a place or region newly settled, or a small village.

2. musket = a large heavy shoulder gun such as a flintlock or a matchlock.

3. heathen savage = an uncivilized, irreligious barbarian.

4. timidly = lacking in courage or self-confidence or boldness. Shyly.

5. fearful = full of fear, afraid.

Questions:

1 through 8. Answers will vary, but each child should have explainable and/or logical reasons for his or her answers.

Chapters 3 & 4

Vocabulary:

Their definitions may vary.

1. solemn = somber, gloomy, serious.

2. coarse = large, rough texture.

3. fair = pleasing to the eye and mind. Fresh and charming, beautiful.

4. hollowed = having an indentation, cavity or hole.

5. odor = a smell

6. wove = to have interlaced threads or yarn to make cloth

Questions:

1. Answers will vary.

2. He said she was too wise for her years because she realized that Mistress Robinson was not a loving mother, and theirs was not a loving family.

3. He loved Sarah and decided to grant her request.

4. Be careful what you say to others.

5. She felt safe when she was with her father and began talking to him to keep up her courage.

6. Answers will vary.

7. Answers will vary.

Chapters 5 & 6

Vocabulary:

1. namesake, a.

2. mild, b.

3. palisade, b.

4. petticoat, a.

5. serious, a.

6. mortar and pestle, b.

Questions:

1. She got her Bible out to read.

2. Answers will vary.

3. They were curious.

4. She started to read aloud from the Bible.

5. She is sorry that she frightened the Indian children away.

6. Answers will vary.

7. Answers will vary.

8. Answers will vary.

Word Pictures:

1. *as still as* a rabbit in danger.

2. *Like* small brown field mice.

3. *Like* the deer when her father lifted the gun,

4. *like* red jewels in the grass.

Chapters 7 & 8

Vocabulary:

1. c; 2. a; 3. b; 4. e; 5. d

Questions:

1. Answers will vary. The Indians apparently feared an attack by the Indians from the north.

2. "To be afraid and to be brave is the best courage of all," said her father.

3. She worried that something might happen to her father, that he might not return and she would have to live with the Indians all her life.

4. Answers will vary.

5. Tall John held her hand, and then he carried her on his shoulder to his house.

6. Answers will vary. The simile is: "like the silk on the corn in late summer."

7. Her father was not there to listen to her prayers this time.

8. Answers will vary.

Chapters 9, 10 & 11

Vocabulary:

1. a drop of water, moisture, wetness on grass or the ground
2. a ruckus, worry, problems
3. sweet, nice, interesting, wonderful
4. happy, thinking something is funny
5. hard, unbending
6. a bother, tiring, boring, a chore
7. fussy, whimpering, crying
8. strange, alien, unusual, different
9. strange, weird, odd, different
10. robbed, attacked

Questions:

1. They thought the Indians from the north were coming.
2. A fold of her cloak. To encourage and comfort herself.
3. Indian men kept watch on hills all along the Great River.
4. A wolf.
5. Guessing what shoe a pebble was in.
6. He would miss Sarah. He loved her like a daughter.
7. Answers will vary.
8. Answers will vary.
9. Answers will vary.
10. A fight, argument, disagreement, scolding.
11. Answers will vary.
12. She was with her mother and her entire family again.
13. Answers will vary.

Crossword Puzzle

Across:

2. Once she seemed to hear a long, low wailing. Was this the _signal_?
4. Sarah _waited_ for her father to speak.
6. They came at sundown to a _settlement_.
10. "Tonight we do not need to eat that dry _johnnycake_," Sarah said.
11. She had kept up her _courage_ and it was something that would always be with her.
13. Were the _Indians_ coming down from the North?
14. Suppose . . . Suppose . . . But tired from long days in the sun she slept at last, always with a fold of her _cloak_ caught in her hand.

Down:

1. That she would have to see for herself—if she could even bring herself to look into one of those queer _wigwams_.
3. So they were walking, all three of them, when they came to the _cabin_ where the candle wood was lighted early.
5. The _latch_ was lifted and a woman stood in the doorway looking at them.
7. They _traded_ with the Indians for corn, and ground it with the small mortar and pestle Thomas had brought in one of the saddle bags.
8. She also made a pair of deerskin _moccasins_.
9. It had been a long day, and the _trail_ through the forest had not been easy.
10. The frost was on the ground when Sarah stood, holding Tall John's hand, to watch her father start on his _journey_.
12. Tall John's wife taught Sarah how to weave a _basket_.